Scholastic Success With
Fluency

Grade 4

by Linda Van Vickle

New York • Toronto • London • Auckland • Sydney **Teaching**
Mexico City • New Delhi • Hong Kong • Buenos Aires *Resources*

Cover art by Amy Vangsgard
Cover design by Maria Lilja
Interior illustrations by Mike Denman
Interior design by Quack & Company

ISBN 0-439-55388-1

Copyright © 2004 Scholastic, Inc.
All rights reserved. Printed in the U.S.A.

2 3 4 5 6 7 8 9 10   40   09 08 07 06 05 04

Introduction

Parents and teachers alike will find this book a valuable tool in helping students become fluent readers. Fluency is the ability to read smoothly and easily and is essential to reading comprehension. Prereading activities, which include building vocabulary and context, help students prepare for the readings. Decoding words ahead of time enables students to focus more attention on the actual meaning of the text. Activities are also designed to help students build their reading speed. By training their eyes to read more than one word at a time, students stay more focused and can better remember what they have read. This book also encourages students to read aloud with expression, which helps foster better comprehension. Students demonstrate their understanding of the readings in follow-up exercises and then extend this understanding through critical thinking questions. You will feel rewarded providing such a valuable resource for your students. Remember to praise them for their efforts and successes!

Table of Contents

Leafy Jaws

 Building Vocabulary—*Sometimes a story or a chapter in a textbook may have so many new words that you hardly understand what you have just read. One of the ways to become a better reader is to know and understand all the words you come across as you read. Then practice reading the words aloud.*

Look at the following words found in the story "Leafy Jaws." Each word is a noun that names an animal. Match each word with the picture of the animal it names.

_____ shark

_____ tarantula

_____ grizzly bear

_____ crocodile

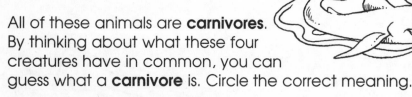

All of these animals are **carnivores**. By thinking about what these four creatures have in common, you can guess what a **carnivore** is. Circle the correct meaning.

a. an animal that has fur

b. an animal that kills and eats other creatures

c. an animal that can swim

d. an animal that has sharp claws and teeth

Here are some of the other nouns you will find in the article. Match each word with its definition. Some of the words you may already know. Look for clues in the definitions to help you understand the words you do not know.

1. _____ a sweet liquid secreted by flowers   **a.** botanist

2. _____ a small container in which plants are grown   **b.** diameter

3. _____ one who studies plants   **c.** exoskeleton

4. _____ places where young plants are grown for sale   **d.** habitat

5. _____ the width of a circle   **e.** nectar

6. _____ a creature hunted or caught for food   **f.** nurseries

7. _____ a place where a creature lives   **g.** prey

8. _____ an external supporting structure of insects   **h.** terrarium

cle the letter of the word or phrase that best explains the meaning of the underlined jective in each sentence. Use your understanding of the nouns to help figure out the meanings.

1. A <u>reputable</u> nursery will sell only healthy plants.
   a. famous
   b. honest
   c. large

2. A Venus flytrap is an <u>endangered</u> species in the wild.
   a. Its survival is threatened.
   b. It is fierce and mean.
   c. There are too many.

3. <u>Domestic</u> plants are grown in terrariums rather than their natural habitat.
   a. leafy and green
   b. raised by people
   c. healthy

4. A <u>carnivorous</u> plant eats insects.
   a. big and hairy
   b. able to live on land and sea
   c. able to catch, kill, and eat prey

Use your understanding of the nouns and adjectives to help figure out the meanings of some of the verbs you will be reading. Complete the sentences with the correct verbs.

detect   devours   doubted

secretes   supplements

The carnivorous Venus flytrap _____ the nutrients it receives from

the soil with the insects it captures and _____. To attract insects, the

plant _____ a sweet nectar. When its leaves _____ an

insect has landed on them, they close up and trap the prey. The Venus flytrap is

such an amazing plant that botanists at first _____ its existence.

Practice reading words from the story. Read through the chart several times, trying to read a little faster each time.

crocodile	supplements	nectar	prey	terrarium	domestic	reputable
carnivorous	exoskeleton	botanist	shark	doubted	devours	diameter
grizzly bear	endangered	habitat	detect	nurseries	secretes	tarantula

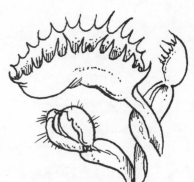

Reading the Story

Carnivorous creatures are those that can capture, kill, and digest insects or other animal life. Carnivorous creatures include crocodiles, grizzly bears, sharks, tarantulas, and Venus flytraps. You might have expected there to be carnivorous reptiles, mammals, fish, and insects. But did you expect to find a plant on the list of carnivores? Even early botanists doubted that such a plant could exist, but the Venus flytrap is a true carnivore that captures its insect meals in its leafy jaws.

The Venus flytrap is native to the sunny bogs and wetlands of North and South Carolina. Since the soil in this region is too poor to meet the plant's needs, it supplements its diet with the minerals it gets by devouring insects. A mature Venus flytrap is usually about six inches in diameter, and the four to eight "traps" at the end of its leaves are about one inch long. Small flies, spiders, and crickets are the typical "prey" of a Venus flytrap.

To attract prey, the leaves forming the trap secrete a sweet nectar. When an insect lands on or climbs in the trap, it brushes against tiny "trigger" hairs inside the trap. When these hairs detect motion, the leaves of the trap can tightly shut within half a second. The plant then begins secreting digestive juices that dissolve the insect, so its nutrients can be absorbed. In about five to twelve days, the trap reopens, and all that remains of the insect is its shell or exoskeleton, which blows away. Each of the leafy traps can close only a limited number of times. Once this limit is reached, the trap eventually dies and falls away, and the plant grows new traps to replace it.

Today, the Venus flytraps growing in the wild are endangered because of the destruction of their native wetlands, pollution, and over-collection. There are strict fines for taking them out of their habitat in the Carolinas. However, you can obtain domestic Venus flytraps from reputable plant nurseries. A carefully set-up and maintained terrarium can duplicate the sunny, humid, moist growing conditions the Venus flytrap needs in order to grow. You also have to provide your plant with crickets and other small insects. Sometimes well-meaning growers will try to feed their Venus flytrap hamburger. The leaves were not designed to catch cows, and trying to feed the plant hamburger will only kill it. Remember, too, that the traps can only open and close so many times. Poking its leaves with a pencil to make the traps snap shut may cause the traps to wear out and die before the plant can grow new ones. With the right care and growing conditions, the Venus flytrap will be a fascinating addition to your in-home garden.

Thinking About What You Read

1. Why do you think botanists doubted that the Venus flytrap existed?

_____

_____

_____

2. You learned the process the Venus flytrap uses to attract, trap, and devour its prey. Complete the following summary of that process by adding the correct words.

First, the plant attracts insects by secreting a sweet __ __ __ __ __ __.

When the flytrap's trigger hairs __ __ __ __ __ __ motion, they close up on the insect.

The plant then __ __ __ __ __ __ __ __ digestive juices that dissolve the insect.

When the leaves open in five to twelve days, all that remains is the insect's

__ __ __ __ __ __ __ __ __ __ __.

3. Circle the correct answers about owning a Venus flytrap.

You should get your Venus flytrap by

    a. going to the Carolinas and digging it up.

    b. ordering one from a reputable nursery.

You should grow the Venus flytrap

    a. in a terrarium that duplicates the plant's natural habitat.

    b. in your backyard.

You should feed the Venus flytrap

    a. crickets.

    b. hamburger.

A Giant Hoax

 Building Vocabulary

Have you ever heard the expression a get-rich-quick scheme? A scheme is a plan or plot to do something. A get-rich-quick scheme, then, is a plan to make a lot of money in a short period of time. Usually, these kinds of schemes are not very honest. You are going to read the story of a man who fooled thousands of people with just such a scheme.

Here are some of the words you will find as you read about the famous get-rich-quick scheme of George Hull. Practice reading the chart several times, trying to read it a little faster each time.

hoax	prankster	authentic	petrified	pores	secrecy
fake	exhibition	admission	patient	lawsuit	ancient

To make sure you know the meanings of the words, complete the puzzle. Use a dictionary to help you.

Across

1. not real, a counterfeit
3. one who plays tricks
4. very old
5. a case brought before a court
7. state of being kept hidden
9. a trick or practical joke
11. turned to stone
12. able to wait for the right moment

Down

2. genuine, real
6. tiny holes in the skin
8. a display for the public
10. an entrance fee

Scholastic Teaching Resources

Reading the Story—*Reading a story more than once is an excellent way to improve reading fluency. It is also important to practice reading aloud as well as silently. Often when reading silently, a reader may mispronounce or skip words. This can interfere with reading comprehension. Read the following story aloud. Review any words you have difficulty pronouncing.*

George Hull was a cigar-maker who was always on the lookout for get-rich-quick schemes. When he heard a preacher say that giants once walked the earth, Hull decided to make that the focus of what has been called "America's greatest hoax."

In 1868 Hull had a master stonecutter carve a statue of a giant from a special rock. Working in secrecy, the stonecutter and his assistants carved a massive ten-foot, 3,000-pound giant. Its details were very lifelike. The giant even had authentic-looking skin pores.

Hull had the giant shipped to a relative's farm in Cardiff, New York. Late one night, Hull and a relative buried the giant in a marshy area. Hull was a patient prankster and waited about a year to begin the next stage of his hoax. In 1869 he told his relative to hire workmen to dig a well where the giant was buried. As expected, the workmen discovered the giant "petrified man," and news of its discovery soon spread. A tent was set up over the pit where the giant lay, and people paid fifty cents for a look at the giant.

Soon thousands of people from all over the country arrived every day to see the Cardiff Giant. Scientists and professors, too, came and examined the giant. Some said it truly was a petrified man. Others believed it was an ancient statue. There were those who said the giant was a hoax, but the crowds kept coming. Hull sold the giant to a group of businessmen, who moved it to Syracuse, New York, for exhibition. There a paleontologist declared it a fake. Hull then admitted that the Cardiff Giant was a hoax, but the crowds kept coming anyway.

The great circus showman P.T. Barnum tried to buy the giant, and when his offer was turned down, he had workmen carve another giant out of wood. He then began showing his own giant calling it a fake of a fake. The businessmen brought a lawsuit against Barnum for calling their giant a fake. The judge refused to hear the case unless the original Cardiff Giant could be proven real. The businessmen dropped the charges.

For a while, crowds of people still paid to view the giants, with Barnum's fake giant drawing bigger crowds than the original Cardiff Giant.

Today, the original Cardiff Giant can be seen at the Farmers' Museum in Cooperstown, New York.

Sequencing the Information

Number the events in the order they happened in the story.

_____ **Thousands of people came to view the giant.**

_____ **P.T. Barnum tried to buy the Cardiff Giant.**

_____ **George Hull hired a stonecutter to carve a statue of a giant.**

_____ **Workmen discovered a "petrified man."**

_____ **The giant was moved to Syracuse, New York.**

_____ **George Hull admitted the Cardiff Giant was a fake.**

_____ **Hull and a relative buried the statue in a marshy area.**

_____ **P.T. Barnum hired workmen to carve a giant out of wood.**

_____ **Workmen were hired to dig a well.**

Before rereading "A Giant Hoax," look over the questions on page 11. As you reread, look for clues to help you answer the questions.

Scholastic Teaching Resources

➤ **Thinking About What You Read**

1. George Hull probably had more than one reason for going through all the work to create this hoax. What are some reasons you think he did this?

   _____

   _____

   _____

   _____

2. Why do you think so many people, even educated professors, were fooled by Hull's giant?

   _____

   _____

   _____

   _____

3. Even after both giants were revealed to be fake, people still paid to see them! Why do you think more people went to see Barnum's fake giant rather than the original fake giant?

   _____

   _____

   _____

4. Many have said that there is a fool born every minute. Do you agree or disagree? Use details from the story to support your answer.

   _____

   _____

   _____

   _____

   _____

High and Low

 Building Context

You can become a better reader by taking some time before you read to think about what you already know about the subject of the article or story. Learning new information is easier if you can connect it to what you already know.

You are going to read an article about the highest and lowest places on our planet: Mount Everest and the Marianas Trench. Think about what you already know or think you know about these two places.

Have you ever heard of Mount Everest? If so, write down any facts or details you know about this mountain. If you have never heard of it, write down what you think it would be like on the very top of the highest mountain in the world.

_____

_____

_____

_____

How do you think you would reach the top of the highest mountain in the world? What dangers would you face? How long do you think it would take to reach the top?

_____

_____

_____

_____

Now think about the deepest part of the ocean. How far down do you think it is? How would you get there? Do you think you could swim there if you had oxygen tanks? Would you find any fish at this depth? Write down any ideas you have about what the journey would be like and what you would find at the bottom of the ocean.

_____

_____

_____

_____

Building Vocabulary

There are several proper nouns in the article about the highest and lowest points on earth. While you may not have known these words if you just saw them in isolation, if you think about them in the context of what you are going to read, their meanings are easier to figure out.

Listed below are the proper nouns that tell about the highest place on earth. Complete the sentences that follow with the correct proper nouns.

Sir Edmund Hillary   Base Camp   Himalayan Mountains   Mount Everest

The _____ make up a mountain range that extends

1,500 miles through south-central Asia. _____ is the highest

peak in this range and the highest point on earth. The mountain is so high that

climbers must spend several weeks at _____ before their

bodies are adjusted to the high altitude and they can attempt the climb. The first

person to reach the top of this great mountain was _____.

Listed below are the proper nouns that tell about the lowest point on earth. Complete the sentences that follow with the correct proper nouns.

Challenger Deep   Pacific   U.S. Navy

Marianas Trench   *Trieste*   Philippine Islands

Philippines

The _____ Ocean is the largest and deepest ocean in the

world. Its deepest point is found just east of the _____ in a

deep underwater canyon called the _____. A British survey

ship called Challenger II found the deepest point in this canyon. This point was

named _____. In 1960 the _____ sent a

two-man mini-submarine, named the _____ , to this deepest

point.

Make a Prediction: Two men reached the lowest point on earth in 1960. Do you think the first man stood at the highest point on earth before or after 1960? _____ Read "High and Low" to see if you are correct.

Building Speed—*Once a good base of context and vocabulary is established, it is time to start reading. Good readers know that they will have to read a story several times to fully understand it. The first reading should be done quickly to provide a general understanding of the story.*

One way to read quickly is to train the eyes to look at more than one word at a time. Reading each word individually is like watching a movie in slow motion. Eventually the brain gets bored, and the mind wanders. Reading chunks of words will help you read faster and stay focused on what is being read.

For this practice, "High and Low" has been broken down into "chunks," first to help you read faster and then to help you think about what you have read. As you read, try to read each word group and then go on to the next group, pausing after the double lines. Avoid rereading the same words because that will slow you down.

High and Low

Imagine that/ you wanted to visit/ the highest/ and the lowest/ places on earth.// Where would you go?// How would you/ get there?// What would you/ find there?//

To get to the highest point/ in the world/ you would have to journey/ to the Himalayan Mountains.// In this mountain range/ in Asia,/ you would find Mount Everest.// At over 29,000 feet,/ it is the highest point/ on the planet.// Since Sir Edmund Hillary/ was the first/ to reach the summit/ of Mount Everest in 1953,/ more than 600 people/ have stood/ at the top of the world.// But your trip/ would not be easy.//

Why would the trip to the top of the world not be easy? _____

_____

_____

Before attempting/ to climb Mount Everest,/ you would have to spend several weeks/ at Base Camp.// Base Camp sits/ at 17,700 feet.// You would have to stay there/ until your body adjusted/ to the lower pressure/ of oxygen at high altitudes.// If you tried to/ climb Everest/ without doing this,/ you would pass out and die.// Once you left Base Camp,/ your climb/ would take several more weeks.// The weather on Mount Everest/ is unpredictable.// You could be caught/ in fierce winds,/ reaching 177 miles per hour,/ or in fierce snowstorms,/ dropping up to/ ten feet of snow.// There is also the danger/ of avalanches and falling ice.// If you were one of the lucky ones/ to make it to the summit,/ you would have/ a magnificent view/ of snow-capped mountains.// You would look down/ upon the tops of clouds/ and up into a dark blue sky.//

Scholastic Teaching Resources

Why is it important to spend several weeks at Base Camp before attempting to climb the mountain? _____

_____

_____

The trip to the lowest place/ on earth/ would be a very/ different journey.// First, you would have/ to take a boat/ to a point in the Pacific Ocean/ just east of/ the Philippine Islands.// There, almost 36,000 below/ the surface of the ocean,/ is Challenger Deep,/ the lowest point/ on the planet.// The water there is deeper than/ Mount Everest is high.// Challenger Deep/ is part of the Marianas Trench,/ a long canyon/ on the ocean floor.// Visiting the lowest point on earth/ is also not easy.//

List ways the journey to the lowest point on earth may be different from the journey to the highest point. _____

_____

_____

With almost seven miles of water/ over your head,/ you would need protection/ from the tremendous pressure.// You would have to make/ your journey/ in a specially-built mini-submarine,/ such as the *Trieste,*/ sent down to the ocean floor/ by the U.S. Navy/ in 1960.// Like the two-man crew/ of the *Trieste,*/ you would spend/ more than four hours/ dropping down/ into total darkness.// No light reaches/ these depths.// Your vessel would shake/ and groan/ under the extreme pressure.// When you hit bottom,/ you would be in icy darkness.// But, surprisingly,/ you would not be alone.// Even at this depth,/ the ocean floor/ is alive with small creatures.//

Brave adventurers/ have already visited/ the highest and lowest points/ on earth.// Would you be willing/ to face the dangers/ of these journeys?

What are some of the characteristics you think the small creatures found on the ocean floor have? _____

_____

_____

Reading the Story

Imagine that you wanted to visit the highest and the lowest places on earth. Where would you go? How would you get there? What would you find there?

To get to the highest point in the world you would have to journey to the Himalayan Mountains. In this mountain range in Asia, you would find Mount Everest. At over 29,000 feet, it is the highest point on the planet. Since Sir Edmund Hillary was the first to reach the summit of Mount Everest in 1953, more than 600 people have stood at the top of the world. But your trip would not be easy.

Before attempting to climb Mount Everest, you would have to spend several weeks at Base Camp. Base Camp sits at 17,700 feet. You would have to stay there until your body adjusted to the lower pressure of oxygen at high altitudes. If you tried to climb Everest without doing this, you would pass out and die. Once you left Base Camp, your climb would take several more weeks. The weather on Mount Everest is unpredictable. You could be caught in fierce winds, reaching 177 miles per hour, or in fierce snowstorms, dropping up to ten feet of snow. There is also the danger of avalanches and falling ice. If you were one of the lucky ones to make it to the summit, you would have a

magnificent view of snow-capped mountains. You would look down upon the tops of clouds and up into a dark blue sky.

The trip to the lowest place on earth would be a very different journey. First, you would have to take a boat to a point in the Pacific Ocean just east of the Philippine Islands. There, almost 36,000 below the surface of the ocean, is Challenger Deep, the lowest point on the planet. The water there is deeper than Mount Everest is high. Challenger Deep is part of the Marianas Trench, a long canyon on the ocean floor. Visiting the lowest point on earth is also not easy.

With almost seven miles of water over your head, you would need protection from the tremendous pressure. You would have to make your journey in a specially-built mini-submarine, such as the *Trieste*, sent down to the lowest point by the U.S. Navy in 1960. Like the two-man crew of the *Trieste*, you would spend more than four hours dropping down into total darkness. No light reaches these depths. Your vessel would shake and groan under the extreme pressure. When you hit bottom, you would be in icy darkness. But, surprisingly, you would not be alone. Even at this depth, the ocean floor is alive with small creatures.

Brave adventurers have already visited the highest and lowest points on earth. Would you be willing to face the dangers of these journeys?

Thinking About What You Read

1. **Explain which of the two journeys you think is the most dangerous and why.**

   _____

   _____

   _____

   _____

2. **Which place would you be most interested in seeing? Why?**

   _____

   _____

   _____

3. **What are some other dangerous explorations human beings have made? What discoveries do you think lie ahead?**

   _____

   _____

   _____

   _____

Towering Tribute

 Building Context and Vocabulary

You will better understand the story of the Crazy Horse Monument if you know something about the people and places in the story.

Lakota: This is one of the Native American tribes that made up the Sioux nation, a people who lived and hunted in the Great Plains of what are now the Dakotas, Minnesota, and Nebraska. Settlers and soldiers killed nearly all the buffalo and forced the Sioux from their homelands onto reservations, land set aside for Native Americans by the U.S. government.

Black Hills: This is a mountainous region in southwestern South Dakota.

Mount Rushmore: This mountain in the Black Hills is a national memorial, famous for its sixty-foot-high carvings of the heads and faces of presidents George Washington, Thomas Jefferson, Abraham Lincoln, and Theodore Roosevelt.

Crazy Horse: He was a Lakota Sioux chief, considered a great leader and warrior by his people. He tried to keep his people from being sent to reservations by hiding out with them in the Black Hills. Eventually, he was forced to surrender. He was killed by government soldiers.

Korcsak Ziolkowski (kor-chok jewel-CUFF-ski): He was an American sculptor who spent nearly 36 years carving a mountain in the Black Hills into a monument to honor the spirit of Crazy Horse and his people. Today, his children continue to work on the massive monument.

Using all five of the above proper nouns, tell in at least three sentences why you think the Black Hills is a good site for the Crazy Horse Monument.

_____

_____

_____

_____

_____

_____

_____

Building Vocabulary

You know that you can read faster and understand more of what you read if you are familiar with the words in a story or passage. Practicing reading the words helps you even more.

Before you begin a careful reading of "Towering Tribute," take a few minutes to skim through the story. Underline words that might slow you down because you do not know their meanings or how to pronounce them.

Add the words that you most want to practice to the chart below. Practice reading the words in the chart aloud several times, trying to read them a little faster each time.

Crazy Horse			
	Mount Rushmore		
		Black Hills	
			Lakota
	Ziolkowski		

Are there any words that you do not know? List those words below and then look them up in a dictionary. Write a short definition next to each word.

_____   _____

_____   _____

_____   _____

_____   _____

_____   _____

_____   _____

After practicing reading these words and making sure you know their meanings, carefully read "Towering Tribute."

 **Reading the Story**

Crazy Horse was a great leader of the Lakota who defended his people and their way of life. A fearless warrior, Crazy Horse led many successful battles against the settlers and soldiers who tried to take his tribe's lands. In 1876, when the U.S. government ordered all the Lakota tribes onto reservations, Crazy Horse resisted. He led his people into the Black Hills, and for months they evaded the soldiers that were sent to capture them. Only when disease and hunger weakened his people did

Crazy Horse surrender. Even in defeat, Crazy Horse remained proud and independent in spirit. When Crazy Horse left the reservation to seek help for his sick wife, soldiers feared he was plotting a return to battle and ordered his arrest. At first Crazy Horse did not resist, but when he realized the soldiers were taking him to a guardhouse, he struggled and was stabbed with a bayonet. On September 6, 1877, Crazy Horse died.

On that same day, 31 years later, the man who would pay Crazy Horse and all Native Americans a great tribute, Korcsak Ziolkowski, was born. He became a well-known sculptor. He even assisted with the work of carving the statues on Mount Rushmore. After World War II, Ziolkowski accepted the invitation of Sioux Indian chiefs to create a monument to Crazy Horse in the Black Hills. For his sculpture, Ziolkowski chose a 600-foot mountain! In 1946 Ziolkowski created a much smaller sculpture of Crazy Horse made from Tennessee marble, to serve as a model. Two years later, beginning his work with a jackhammer and dynamite, Ziolkowski took ten tons of rock off the mountain.

Ziolkowski knew that carving a sculpture the size of a mountain would take dedication and more than a lifetime's work. He spent the rest of his life working on the monument, never accepting a salary. He also refused to take any government money and used only private donations and admission charges to cover expenses. When Ziolkowski died in 1982, his wife and seven of his children continued his dream to turn the mountain into a monument. In 1998 the face of Crazy Horse was completed and a dedication ceremony was held on the 50th anniversary of the first dynamite blast.

No one knows how long it will take to finish the Crazy Horse Monument, but when it is finished, it will be the largest statue in the world, 563 feet high and 641 feet long. It will be a towering tribute to Crazy Horse, a great Native American hero, and to his people.

Thinking About What You Read

1. Crazy Horse was very proud and independent. He never allowed his picture to be taken, so no one knows what he looked like. Do you think it matters that the statue does not look like the real Crazy Horse? Why or why not?

_____

_____

_____

_____

2. No government money was ever used in the construction of the Crazy Horse Monument. Why do you think Ziolkowski insisted upon this?

_____

_____

_____

_____

3. Ziolkowski worked on carving the Crazy Horse Monument for nearly 36 years, and since his death, his children have continued the work. Why do you think a man would start a project too big to complete in his lifetime?

_____

_____

_____

_____

4. Why do you think Ziolkowski's children have continued his work?

_____

_____

_____

5. Do you think Crazy Horse would approve of his monument? Why or why not?

_____

_____

_____

The Queen of Baseball

 Building Context and Vocabulary

You are going to read the story of a baseball player whom some consider a pioneer in the game. Before reading the whole story, practice reading some of the words you will encounter. Practice reading the list several times, trying to read a little faster each time.

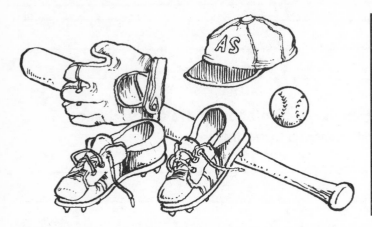

American League	semipro team
charity game	major league
exhibition game	manager
National League	base stealers
player's strike	steal signals
amateur team	first base

Think about the steps that a person has to take in building a career in baseball. Here are the steps the player you are going to read about went through. Number them in the order in which you think they occurred.

_____ **played with friends on weekends after work**

_____ **played with amateur teams**

_____ **played with Dad and brother**

_____ **played in a major league exhibition game**

_____ **played with semipro teams**

The ballplayer in this story played baseball throughout the New England states and in eastern Canada. Because her mother was French-Canadian, this ballplayer could speak *fluent* French as well as English. *Fluent* means she could speak and understand the language as well as a native speaker. Do you think speaking French could help this ballplayer? Explain why or why not.

_____

_____

_____

_____

Scholastic Teaching Resources

 Building Speed

Imagine if every time you took a step, you paused and thought, "I am taking a step. Now I am taking another step." Take a step, pause and think. Take a step, pause and think. Can you imagine how long it would take you to get anywhere? Would you also get pretty bored along the way?

Now think about what happens when you read if you read only one word at a time. You read one word and then pause and think what the word means. Then you read the next word and pause and so on. Reading becomes very slow and boring.

One of the keys to becoming a better reader is to become a faster reader. By training your eyes to see and your brain to process the meaning of more than one word at a time, you will read faster. You will also more likely stay interested in what you are reading.

Practice reading several words at a time as you learn about a young woman who loved baseball and who made it her career.

Mary Elizabeth Murphy
loved to play baseball.
From the time
she was a little girl,
Lizzie, as she was called,
played ball
with her brother and her dad.
Her dream was
to be a baseball player.
While today Lizzie's dream
may not seem so unusual,
Lizzie was born in 1894.
She grew up
during a time when
women wore long skirts,
and most chose careers
as wives, mothers,
housekeepers, or teachers.
Women did not even have
the right to vote in most states.

When Lizzie was 12 years old,
she went to work
in the woolens mill,
but she did not
give up her dream.
She played every chance she could
after work and on weekends.
By age 15,
she had been playing baseball
for a number of amateur teams
when she caught the attention
of the manager of a semipro team
in Rhode Island.
He offered her five dollars a game
and her share of the "take"
when the team would pass a hat
through the crowd for donations.
Lizzie accepted his offer.
A big crowd showed up
at her first game,

curious to see how
a woman could play first base.
The take that night was $85,
but the manager refused
to give Lizzie her share
and even her five-dollar salary.
The following week
when the team was boarding the bus
for a game in Newport,
Lizzie refused to go with the team
unless she was paid
what she was promised.
Her "player's strike" was successful,
and from then on,
the manager always paid her.

Lizzie kept improving as a player.
In 1918 she was signed
by a semipro team,
Ed Carr's All-Stars of Boston.
For the next 17 years,
Lizzie earned her living
as a first-base player.
She played 100 games each summer,
traveling with her team
throughout New England
and eastern Canada.
During one game in Canada,
Lizzie overheard
the first-base coach
discussing steal signals
with a runner in French.
Lizzie happened to speak
fluent French
but did not let on
that she understood.
She called a time-out

and set up a series of signals
with the catcher
to let him know when
someone was going to steal.
They caught five base stealers
during that game.

In 1922 the Boston Red Sox
played a charity game
against a team made up of
American League players
and the All-Stars.
Lizzie was chosen by the All-Stars
to play first base.
Six years later, she played
in a major league exhibition game
between the National League All-Stars
and the Boston Braves.
She was the first woman
to play for a major league team
in an exhibition game
and is said to have been
the first person to play with
both American and National League
All-Star teams.
Lizzie Murphy truly was
        the "Queen of Baseball."

➡️ **Thinking About What You Read**

1. How did your eyes move when you read the story broken down into short lines? Were you able to read the entire line at once?

_____

_____

_____

_____

2. Did you predict the correct order of steps that Lizzie Murphy went through in her baseball career? What did you know about baseball before reading this story that might have helped you?

_____

_____

_____

_____

3. Do you think it was fair that Lizzie did not tell the other team's first-base coach that she could speak French and knew all of his secret steal signals? Why or why not?

_____

_____

_____

_____

4. What did you find most interesting or most surprising about the story of Lizzie Murphy?

_____

_____

_____

_____

Now read the story again in a regular story form. As you read, continue to try to scan more than one word at a time. Notice if you are able to read the story a little faster with practice.

Name _____

 The Queen of Baseball

 Reading the Story

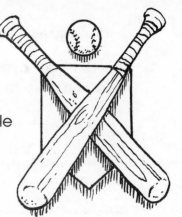

Mary Elizabeth Murphy loved to play baseball. From the time she was a little girl, Lizzie, as she was called, played ball with her brother and her dad. Her dream was to be a baseball player. While today Lizzie's dream may not seem so unusual, Lizzie was born in 1894. She grew up during a time when women wore long skirts, and most chose careers as wives, mothers, housekeepers, or teachers. Women did not even have the right to vote in most states.

When Lizzie was 12 years old, she went to work in the woolens mill, but she did not give up her dream. She played every chance she could after work and on weekends. By age 15, she had been playing baseball for a number of amateur teams when she caught the attention of the manager of a semipro team in Rhode Island. He offered her five dollars a game and her share of the "take" when the team would pass a hat through the crowd for donations. Lizzie accepted his offer. A big crowd showed up at her first game, curious to see how a woman could play first base. The take that night was $85, but the manager refused to give Lizzie her share and even her five-dollar salary. The following week when the team was boarding the bus for a game in Newport, Lizzie refused to go with the team unless she was paid what she was promised. Her "player's strike" was successful, and from then on, the manager always paid her.

Lizzie kept improving as a player. In 1918 she was signed by a semipro team, Ed Carr's All-Stars of Boston. For the next 17 years, Lizzie earned her living as a first-base player. She played 100 games each summer, traveling with her team throughout New England and eastern Canada. During one game in Canada, Lizzie overheard the first-base coach discussing steal signals with a runner in French. Lizzie happened to speak fluent French but did not let on that she understood. She called a time-out and set up a series of signals with the catcher to let him know when someone was going to steal. They caught five base stealers during that game.

In 1922 the Boston Red Sox played a charity game against a team made up of American League players and the All-Stars. Lizzie was chosen by the All-Stars to play first base. Six years later, she played in a major league exhibition game between the National League All-Stars and the Boston Braves. She was the first woman to play for a major league team in an exhibition game and is said to have been the first person to play with both American and National League All-Star teams. Lizzie Murphy truly was the "Queen of Baseball."

Scholastic Teaching Resources

Vulture Culture

 Building Vocabulary

As you prepare to read about the turkey vulture, practice reading the following words, which you will encounter in the story. Read the chart through several times, trying to read a little faster each time.

immune	valuable	breakthrough
stork	digestive	threatened
carcass	buzzard	environment
vomit	bacteria	Cherokee
solitary	graceful	scavengers
condor	flamingo	vegetation
pounce	social	featherless
vulture	wingspan	regurgitate

Answer the questions about the words in the chart. Use a dictionary to help you.

1. The names of four birds are listed in the chart. What are they? __ __ __ __ __,
   __ __ __ __ __ __, __ __ __ __ __ __ __ __, and __ __ __ __ __ __ __

2. A synonym is a word that has the same meaning as another word. Which word on the chart is a synonym for *vomit*? __ __ __ __ __ __ __ __ __ __ __

3. An antonym is a word that has the opposite meaning of another word. Which word from the chart is an antonym for *solitary*? __ __ __ __ __ __

4. What do we call animals that feed on the flesh of dead animals?
   __ __ __ __ __ __ __ __ __ __

5. Which of the words from the chart means "body of a dead animal"? __ __ __ __ __ __ __

6. Which of the words from the chart is the name of a Native American tribe?

   __ __ __ __ __ __ __ __

Building Speed

Practice reading faster by trying to scan or read more than one word at a time.

The poor turkey vulture   often gets no respect.   Some people call it a "buzzard"   and say it is dirty   because it feeds   on dead animals. They picture   a solitary bird,   circling overhead,   looking for some weak, dying creature   to pounce on and kill.   Actually, the turkey vulture is graceful, peaceful,   and very social.   It provides a valuable service to our environment   and could hold   the key to some important medical breakthroughs.

The turkey vulture   is not a buzzard.   Like the California condor and the black vulture,   it is more closely related   to storks and flamingos. Like them,   it eats meat,   but a big part of its diet   is vegetation such as grass,   leaves, and seeds.   Adult turkey vultures are brown-black   with featherless, red heads.   With a wingspan of six feet, the turkey vulture   is one of the largest birds   in North America. It can glide for hours   without flapping its long wings   by riding the updrafts in the air currents.   Aircraft pilots   have reported seeing   turkey vultures gliding at 20,000 feet.   Since the turkey vulture   has little strength in its small grasping claws and sharp beak,   it does not kill animals. The Cherokee people   call the turkey vulture "peace eagle" because from a distance,   it looks like an eagle,   but it does not kill. The turkey vulture is so peaceful, that if threatened,   it will roll over and play dead.   If it is still threatened, the turkey vulture   may vomit on its enemy, and the foul odor   usually drives the enemy away.

We probably do not   stop to think about   how many millions of animals die each year.   Yet because of scavengers   like the turkey vulture, we do not have to deal   with the sight and smell   and the threat of disease from all these dead carcasses.

As it soars through the sky,   the turkey vulture   uses its keen vision and smell   to search for animal carcasses.   It can smell a dead animal from more than a mile away.   If a turkey vulture   finds a large carcass, like a dead cow,   it somehow manages   to let other vultures know, and soon a large gathering   will join in the feast.

Scientists are very interested   in the turkey vulture   because its digestive system   can kill any virus and bacteria   in the diseased and decaying carcasses it eats.   Even its droppings   and the pellets of dried hair, bone, and vegetation   that it regurgitates are clean and carry no disease.   Understanding the turkey vulture's immune system   could greatly benefit   medical research.

Read through the article one more time before answering the following question.

As you try to improve your reading speed and understanding, what seems to most help you? Place a check mark by the strategies that you think help you read faster and understand more of what you read.

_____ **practicing reading individual words**

_____ **learning the meanings of words before reading them**

_____ **learning some background about the subject before reading**

_____ **practicing reading word groups instead of individual words**

_____ **reading the same story or article a few times**

Now read the article "Vulture Culture" as it might appear in a book. Try to read the article quickly by reading several words at a time.

Scholastic Teaching Resources

 **Reading the Story**

The poor turkey vulture often gets no respect. Some people call it a "buzzard" and say it is dirty because it feeds on dead animals. They picture a solitary bird, circling overhead, looking for some weak, dying creature to pounce on and kill. Actually, the turkey vulture is graceful, peaceful, and very social. It provides a valuable service to our environment and could hold the key to some important medical breakthroughs.

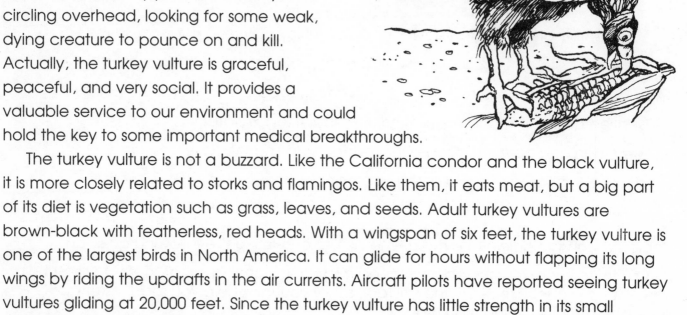

The turkey vulture is not a buzzard. Like the California condor and the black vulture, it is more closely related to storks and flamingos. Like them, it eats meat, but a big part of its diet is vegetation such as grass, leaves, and seeds. Adult turkey vultures are brown-black with featherless, red heads. With a wingspan of six feet, the turkey vulture is one of the largest birds in North America. It can glide for hours without flapping its long wings by riding the updrafts in the air currents. Aircraft pilots have reported seeing turkey vultures gliding at 20,000 feet. Since the turkey vulture has little strength in its small grasping claws and sharp beak, it does not kill animals. The Cherokee people call the turkey vulture "peace eagle" because from a distance, it looks like an eagle, but it does not kill. The turkey vulture is so peaceful, that if threatened, it will roll over and play dead. If it is still threatened, the turkey vulture may vomit on its enemy, and the foul odor usually drives the enemy away.

We probably do not stop to think about how many millions of animals die each year. Yet because of scavengers like the turkey vulture, we do not have to deal with the sight and smell and the threat of disease from all these dead carcasses. As it soars through the sky, the turkey vulture uses its keen vision and smell to search for animal carcasses. It can smell a dead animal from more than a mile away. If a turkey vulture finds a large carcass, like a dead cow, it somehow manages to let other vultures know, and soon a large gathering will join in the feast.

Scientists are very interested in the turkey vulture because its digestive system can kill any virus and bacteria in the diseased and decaying carcasses it eats. Even its droppings and the pellets of dried hair, bone, and vegetation that it regurgitates are clean and carry no disease. Understanding the turkey vulture's immune system could greatly benefit medical research.

Scholastic Teaching Resources

Thinking About What You Read

1. The turkey vulture is a very misunderstood animal. What are some of the misconceptions, or wrong ideas, people have about this bird?

_____

_____

_____

_____

_____

2. The turkey vulture and other scavengers perform what useful service in the environment?

_____

_____

_____

_____

3. The turkey vulture has some amazing abilities. Which did you find the most interesting and why?

_____

_____

_____

_____

4. The turkey vulture is said to be a social animal. What does it mean to be social? Give an example of how the turkey vulture is social.

_____

_____

_____

_____

Tricked by a Monkey

(A Folktale From China)

Building Context and Vocabulary

You are going to read a folktale from China that features two characters often found in Chinese stories: a dragon and a monkey.

Chinese dragons are often found near water. The dragon you will read about lives deep in the ocean with his wife, who is very sick. In many folktales, the monkey is often a clever character who plays tricks. This monkey plays a trick that saves his life.

You will notice in this story that there are a lot of words that describe how the characters talk. Practice reading these words.

groaned	promised	called	answered
begged	asked	cried	said eagerly

To be *eager* is to want to do something very much, so much that you can hardly wait. Think of how you would read something that someone said *eagerly*.

Say aloud, "I want a cookie."

Now say the same sentence *eagerly*: "I want a cookie."

Describe how your voice sounds different when you are *eager*.

_____

_____

Here are some action words that you will also find in the story. Read each one and decide if the words will probably describe an action the dragon does or an action the monkey does. In the space before each word, write *D* for dragon or *M* for monkey.

____ swam   ____ climb   ____ scurried

____ scampered   ____ dived   ____ crawled

 Reading the Story

A dragon lived deep in the ocean with his wife. One day the dragon saw that his wife was very sick. She lay in bed and groaned and moaned and would not eat any food. "You will not get well if you do not eat," the dragon said. "Tell me what you would like, and I will get it for you."

But the dragon's wife just groaned and moaned. The dragon begged his wife to tell him what she would eat. "I promise I will get it for you, no matter what it is," he said.

Finally, the dragon wife moaned, "I would like to eat a monkey's heart."

Since the dragon had promised to get his wife whatever she wanted, he went off in search of a monkey. He swam to the shore of a great jungle and crawled to a grove of tall palm trees. There in the very top of the trees, he saw a monkey. The dragon knew he would have to trick the monkey so it would climb down from the trees.

"Hello, Monkey!" he called. "This is a very nice jungle, but I know where there is a better one."

"How is your jungle better?" the monkey asked.

"In my jungle all the trees are heavy with ripe fruit, more than a monkey could ever eat," answered the dragon. "Hop on my back, and I will take you there."

Quickly, the monkey scurried down the tree and hopped on the dragon's back. "Let's go to your jungle," he said eagerly. "I am very hungry."

But soon the monkey was very afraid and very unhappy. The dragon dived into the ocean and began swimming to the deepest depths.

"Where are we going?" asked the frightened monkey.

"I am sorry that I had to trick you," said the dragon. "My wife is very sick and will only eat a monkey's heart."

"Oh, no!" cried the monkey. "You will have to take me back to land. I left my heart in the treetops!"

The foolish dragon swam quickly back to the shore, where the monkey jumped off his back and scampered high up into the trees. Looking down at the dragon still waiting below, the monkey said to himself, "How stupid dragons must be to believe a story like that!"

Reading With Expression

This folktale has been divided into four parts—the part of the narrator, the dragon, the dragon's wife, and the monkey. Practice reading each part, paying attention to the clues that help you decide how the dialogue should be read.

Narrator: A dragon lived deep in the ocean with his wife. One day the dragon saw that his wife was very sick. She lay in bed and groaned and moaned and would not eat any food.

A narrator can read with expression, too. You are describing a character who is very sick and wants her husband's attention. Your voice can draw out the words "moan" and "groan" to show what a whiney character the dragon's wife is.

Dragon: You will not get well if you do not eat. Tell me what you would like, and I will get it for you.

How should the dragon sound?

　　a. fed up and angry

　　b. happy to help his wife

　　c. worried and trying to help

Narrator: But the dragon's wife just groaned and moaned. The dragon begged his wife to tell him what she would eat.

Dragon: I promise I will get it for you, no matter what it is.

What word clue does the narrator give that tells you how the dragon should sound here?

_____

Narrator: Finally, the dragon's wife moaned.

Dragon's Wife: I would like to eat a monkey's heart.

What word clue does the narrator give that tells you how the dragon's wife should sound here?

_____

Scholastic Teaching Resources

Narrator: Since the dragon had promised to get his wife whatever she wanted, he went off in search of a monkey. He swam to the shore of a great jungle and crawled to a grove of tall palm trees. There in the very top of the trees, he saw a monkey. The dragon knew he would have to trick the monkey so it would climb down from the trees.

Pay attention to commas. Be sure to pause as you read.

Dragon: Hello, Monkey! This is a very nice jungle, but I know where there is a better one.

The dragon is trying to trick the monkey, so how do you think his voice sounds here?

_____

_____

Monkey: How is your jungle better?

Do you think the monkey sounds like he believes the dragon? How might he sound?

_____

_____

Dragon: In my jungle all the trees are heavy with ripe fruit, more than a monkey could ever eat. Hop on my back, and I will take you there.

The dragon is still trying to trick the monkey. Describe how you think he should sound.

_____

_____

Narrator: Quickly, the monkey scurried down the tree and hopped on the dragon's back. Then the monkey spoke eagerly.

Monkey: Let's go to your jungle. I am very hungry.

What word clue does the narrator give that tells you how the monkey should sound here?

_____

Narrator: But soon the monkey was very afraid and very unhappy. The dragon dived into the ocean and began swimming to the deepest depths. The monkey, frightened, asked the dragon a question.

 Here the narrator should try to create some suspense for the reader. The monkey is in real trouble!

Monkey: Where are we going?

 What word clue does the narrator give that tells you how the monkey should sound here?

_____

Dragon: I am sorry that I had to trick you. My wife is very sick and will only eat a monkey's heart.

 What word does the dragon use to tell you how he should sound? _____ Remember, the dragon is a nice guy who wants only to help his wife get better.

Monkey: Oh, no! You will have to take me back to land. I left my heart in the treetops!

 How do you think the monkey should sound here? _____

Narrator: The foolish dragon swam quickly back to the shore, where the monkey jumped off his back and scampered high up into the trees. Looking down at the dragon still waiting below, the monkey spoke quietly to himself.

 The monkey has just had a very close call and barely escaped with his heart. The narrator's voice should help the listeners feel how frightened yet relieved the monkey is to get away.

Monkey: How stupid dragons must be to believe a story like that!

 Now the monkey is safe and feeling very sure of himself. Imagine that as the monkey says this, he is probably rolling his eyes and shaking his head.

Scholastic Teaching Resources

Tooth Tales

> **Previewing and Predicting**

...e title suggests, you are going to read about teeth. Specifically, you are going to learn some interesting facts about the history of tooth care.

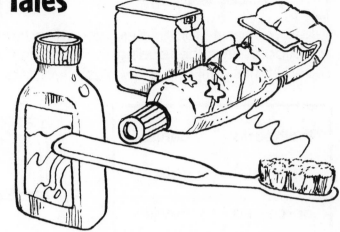

Before you begin reading, think about how we take care of our teeth today and then try to guess how people from long ago tried to take care of their teeth.

When you brush your teeth, you use a toothbrush and toothpaste.

What do you think people used to brush their teeth thousands of years ago?

_____

_____

What do you think they made toothpaste out of back then?

_____

_____

Today, if you need your teeth cleaned or a cavity filled or a tooth pulled, you go to a dentist. Dentists go to school and study many years before they earn a license to practice dentistry.

Whom do you think people went to for dental care hundreds of years ago?

_____

_____

Today, if people lose all their teeth, they can be fitted with very natural-looking dentures made from plastic or ceramic.

What do you think dentures were made out of hundreds of years ago?

_____

_____

When you read "Tooth Tales," see if any of your predictions about what you will learn are correct.

Building Vocabulary

When you read "Tooth Tales," you will encounter a number of words about dentistry and tooth care. Practice reading the words in the box below. Read through the words several times until you know all the words and can read them quickly.

toothpaste	dentists
toothpick	floss
abscessed	cavities
novocaine	dentures
bridgework	decay

Complete the following statements using the words from the chart.

1. **When a tooth is badly infected, and a pocket of fluid builds up around it, the tooth**

   is said to be __ __ __ __ __ __ __ __ __ .

2. **Before pulling a tooth or filling a cavity, the dentist will give the patient a shot of**

   __ __ __ __ __ __ __ __ __ to prevent pain.

3. **Artificial teeth may be attached to the other teeth and gums through**

   __ __ __ __ __ __ __ __ __ __ .

Here are some words that you might not expect to find in a story on tooth care. Guess how each of them might be related to the history of tooth care.

lizard livers _____

hippopotamus ivory _____

chisel and mallet _____

barbers _____

Reading the Story

It is easy to brush and floss our teeth every day. We have our choice of toothpaste flavors and toothbrush sizes and shapes. While a trip to the dentist may make some people nervous, it is usually a pain-free experience. Even having a tooth pulled is nearly painless with a shot of novocaine. Throughout history, people have had to take care of their teeth, but it has not always been this easy or pain-free.

Skulls of people who lived 25,000 years ago show signs of tooth decay. Archaeologists have found evidence of floss and toothpick grooves in these early teeth. The first written notes about dental practices come from a Sumerian text from 5000 B.C. It describes "tooth worms" as the cause of decay. The first known dentist was Hesi-Re, an Egyptian who lived around 2600 B.C. The study of skulls from that period shows that dentists treated tooth problems by pulling teeth and drilling holes in the jawbones to relieve pressure from abscessed teeth.

Toothpaste was used as early as 500 B.C. in China and India. The first toothpastes were made from powdered fruit, ground shells, talc, and honey. The ancient Romans used bones, eggshells, and oyster shells mixed with honey to clean their teeth. Less tasty ingredients in early toothpaste included mice, rabbit heads, and lizard livers. The earliest toothbrushes were just twigs and sticks smashed at one end. Later, bristles from the necks of pigs were used to make toothbrushes. Cavities were filled with small stone chips, turpentine resin, and metals. If a tooth had to come out, the "dentist" used a chisel and mallet.

Who were these early dentists? From the Middle Ages to the early 1700s, the "barber surgeons" cut hair, performed surgeries, and pulled teeth. In fact, in the United States, it was not until 1841 that the first law was passed requiring a dentist to have special training. Until that time, anyone could pull teeth, even fish sellers.

Those people who lost all their teeth to decay and who could afford the high price could have dentures. As early as 700 B.C., false teeth were made out of ivory and bone attached to the gums with gold bridgework. The first U.S. president, George Washington, was a famous denture-wearer. In 1789, when he was sworn into office, Washington had only one natural tooth. His dentist made him a set of dentures. The upper set was made of ivory, and the lower set had eight human teeth fastened by gold pivots screwed into a base made out of hippopotamus ivory. Poor Washington never did find a comfortable-fitting set of dentures. No wonder we never see him smiling in his paintings.

Thinking About the Writer's Purpose

Most writers have a main purpose or reason for writing. Sometimes a writer's purpose is to present information to readers, to teach them something new about a subject. Writers of textbooks often have this purpose: **to inform**. A writer may also just want to present material that entertains the reader because it is interesting or funny. Writers of stories and poems often have this purpose: **to entertain**. Finally, a writer may want to convince readers to think about something in a certain way or to take a specific action. Writers of newspaper editorials often have this purpose: **to persuade**.

The main purpose of "Tooth Tales" is to give you information about the history of tooth care. Writing that informs often includes statements of fact. Complete the following statements using the information you learned from the article.

1. _____, an Egyptian, was the first known dentist.

2. In the year _____, the first law was passed in the United States that required a dentist to have special training.

3. George Washington's dentures had an upper set made out of _____ and a lower set made from eight _____.

The writer presents information in the form of examples as well as facts. Using the information from the article, give examples of each of the following:

4. early ingredients of toothpaste

_____

5. people who could pull teeth in the United States before 1841

_____

What did you think was the most interesting information in this article?

_____

_____

Name _____

Head for Safety

➡ **Building Context**

You are going to be reading an article about bicycle safety. Before you begin reading, think about what is necessary to be a safe bicycle rider.

Write down all that you think a safe bicycle rider should do.

_____

_____

_____

_____

Do you know anyone who has been hurt or injured while riding a bicycle? What do you think causes the most injuries to bicycle riders?

_____

_____

_____

_____

Think about the title of the story you are going to read, "Head for Safety." The word *head* can have two different meanings. One meaning, of course, refers to part of the body. *Head* can also be used as a verb: Let's head over to the library after school.

Which meaning do you think is used in the title of the article? Could both meanings apply? How?

_____

_____

_____

An important piece of safety equipment is the bicycle helmet, yet most young riders do not wear helmets.

Why do you think so many do not wear helmets?

_____

_____

Name _____

Reading the Story

Carrie and Mark love riding their bicycles. Since it will be several years before they can drive cars, Carrie and Mark use their bicycles to get where they need to go. In their small town, they can ride their bikes to most of their friends' houses and to school. Sometimes they hop on their bikes to run errands for their mother. Also, Carrie and Mark both enjoy sports and know that bicycle riding is a good way to stay fit. The exercise they get riding bikes builds up their endurance, so they have the strength and energy they need for baseball, volleyball, and soccer. Best of all, bicycling is just fun. Carrie and Mark love to go on long bike rides with family and friends. Yes, Carrie and Mark love riding bicycles. Unfortunately, every time they ride their bikes, they take a terrible risk. Like 75% of all bike riders under the age of 15, Carrie and Mark do not wear protective helmets.

"I like the feel of the breeze blowing through my hair," says Carrie. "A helmet feels hot and uncomfortable." "I think they look silly," says Mark. But a good bicycle helmet will fit snugly and comfortably on the head. All helmets have ventilation holes to let air through, so they are not hot to wear. Helmets come in a variety of styles and colors, but looking good is not the issue. Safety is what is important. Every year in the United States, 153,000 people are taken to emergency rooms with bicycle-related head injuries. According to the Center for Disease Control, if all bicyclists wore helmets, it would save one life each day and prevent one head injury every four minutes.

"But I am an experienced and careful bike rider," says Mark. No one sets out to have an accident. Even the most experienced and alert bike riders can take a tumble. Mark should note that all Olympic bike riders wear helmets, and they are some of the best and most experienced bikers in the world.

"Helmets are just too expensive," says Carrie. There is a wide range of prices for helmets. Since 1999, all helmets must meet the safety standards set by the Consumer Products Safety Committee. A helmet on sale for under $30 is just as safe as one that sells for $150. When it comes to health and safety, no price is too high, but the cost of a helmet is less than most video games.

Mark and Carrie's arguments against wearing helmets just do not hold up. Let's hope they can be convinced to strap on helmets before the next time they hop on their bikes.

➡ **Thinking About the Writer's Purpose**

1. The writer's main purpose in "Head for Safety" is to persuade the readers to do what?

_____

_____

_____

2. The writer uses some statistics, or numbers, to convince the readers that not wearing helmets is very dangerous. Give an example of a convincing statistic that can be found in the article.

_____

_____

3. Why do you think the writer includes arguments from Carrie and Mark?

_____

_____

_____

4. Complete the following chart to show how the writer matches each of Carrie and Mark's arguments against wearing helmets with reasons that they should wear helmets.

Helmets are hot and uncomfortable.	
Helmets look silly.	
Careful riders do not need helmets.	
Helmets are too expensive.	

Name _____

Battling Brothers

(An African Tale)

➡ **Building Context**

When you hear the word *riches*, what comes to your mind?

_____

_____

_____

_____

Which of these do you think is most valuable? Why?

gold   silver   water   diamonds

_____

_____

_____

Long ago, it was very common in many cultures for a family's wealth to pass to the oldest son. Imagine a family with two sons who do not get along very well. Now imagine that the older son gets all the family's wealth.

How do you think the younger son will feel and act toward his brother?

_____

_____

_____

_____

What do you think will have to happen for the two brothers to finally get along together?

_____

_____

_____

_____

Scholastic Teaching Resources

Reading the Story

Sagbata and Sogbo were two brothers who lived with their mother in a great sky village. Their mother loved both of them and wanted the brothers to rule the world together. But the two brothers were always fighting and could never agree on anything.

One day the older brother, Sagbata, grew so angry, he decided to leave the sky village and live on Earth. "I am the older brother, yet you never listen to me," he said. "I am going down to live on Earth, and I am taking all of our mother's riches with me. Since I am the older son, all the wealth is mine."

"Go away if you wish," replied his brother, Sogbo. "I won't miss you."

Sagbata collected all of his mother's riches and began stuffing them into a large bag. Soon his bag was so full that Sagbata realized he could not take everything with him. "I will leave water behind," he said. It will only soak everything and then leak out of the bag. With his bag filled, Sagbata then began the long journey down to Earth. Once he arrived on Earth, he realized he could never return to the sky again. With his mother's wealth and his power, he soon became king of the village on Earth and was very happy.

Sogbo stayed in the sky with his mother, and soon he was the ruler of the sky village. "Now that I have all the power in the sky village, I will prove to my brother that my power is greater than his," said Sogbo. "Since my brother did not take water with him, it is in my power to keep the rain from falling to Earth." So Sogbo did not allow any rain to fall on Earth for three years. The crops withered, and the people and animals became very thirsty as rivers and streams began to dry up. The people on Earth begged their king, Sagbata, to help them, but there was nothing he could do to make the rains fall.

One day two people from the sky village came down to Earth and visited Sagbata's village. They brought with them magic seeds that could answer any question. Sagbata asked the sky people, "Why is there no rain? How can I help my people?" The sky people threw their seeds on the ground. They looked at the pattern the seeds formed, and then they answered Sagbata's question. The seeds tell us that you have quarreled with your brother. Now you must do what your brother wants if you want him to send rain to your village."

"I am not able to return to the sky village," said Sagbata. "How can I let my brother know that I will give him all my riches in return for water?"

"The Wututu bird is Sogbo's messenger," replied the sky people. "Send him to your brother with an apology and your offer of riches."

Sagbata sent the Wututu bird up to the sky village with this message to his brother. He apologized and offered his brother all of his wealth and power over all the people of the village on Earth. He begged Sogbo to send the rain to Earth.

When Sogbo heard his brother's message, he told the Wututu bird that he would accept his brother's offer. "My brother was foolish to leave water behind. The one who controls water has the greatest power. Now that my brother knows that I am more powerful than he is, I will send rain." Before the Wututu bird could reach the village on Earth with Sogbo's message, the rains began, and the people were saved.

From that day on Sagbata and Sogbo have remained friends, and the rains fall year after year.

Name _____

 Thinking About What You Read

Every culture has folktales, myths, and legends. While these stories can be enjoyed by everyone, knowing something about the culture they come from makes them even more enjoyable and interesting.

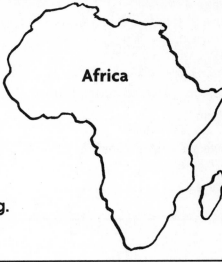

Africa

1. The story of Sagbata and Sogbo comes from the Fon tribe of Western Africa. In this tribe, a queen mother was the highest-ranking ruler followed by one son, who was chosen to be the next heir and the next king. How is this part of the Fon culture shown in the story?

_____

_____

_____

2. The Fon were primarily a farming people. Their land was sometimes hurt by droughts. How is this shown in the story?

_____

_____

_____

3. Many of the tribal peoples of Africa had great respect for animals. How is this shown in the story?

_____

_____

_____

Page 4
3, 4, 2, 1; b; 1. e; 2. h; 3. a; 4. f;
5. b; 6. g; 7. d; 8. c

Page 5
1. b; 2. a; 3. b; 4. c; supplements,
devours, secretes, detect, doubted

Page 7
1. Answers will vary. 2. nectar,
detect, secretes, exoskeleton;
3. b, a, a

Page 8

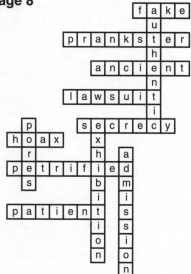

Page 10
5, 8, 1, 4, 6, 7, 2, 9, 3

Page 13
Himalayan Mountains, Mount
Everest, Base Camp, Sir Edmund
Hillary;
Pacific, Philippine Islands, Marianas
Trench, Challenger Deep, U.S. Navy,
Trieste

Page 27
1. stork, condor, buzzard, flamingo;
2. regurgitate; 3. social;
4. scavengers; 5. carcass;
6. Cherokee

Page 31
1. Some people think a turkey
vulture is dirty because it feeds on
dead animals. They also think it is a
solitary bird looking to kill weak,
dying creatures. 2. They eat dead
carcasses which smell and could
spread disease. 3. Answers will vary.
Possible answers include:
It can glide for hours without flapping
its wings. If threatened, it can play
dead or vomit on its enemy. It has
keen vision and smell. Its digestive
system can kill any virus and
bacteria. 4. Social means to enjoy
being in a group. When the turkey
vulture finds a dead animal, it lets
other vultures know. They feast on
the dead animal altogether.

Page 34
c; begged; moaned

Page 35
The dragon should sound confident
and convincing. yes, curious; eagerly

Page 36
frightened; sorry; worried

Page 38
1. abscessed; 2. novocaine;
3. bridgework

Page 40
1. Hesi-Re; 2. 1841; 3. ivory, human
teeth; 4. powdered fruit, ground
shells, talc, honey, bones, eggshells,
oyster shells mixed with honey, mice,
rabbit heads, lizard livers; 5. barbers
and anyone, even fish sellers

Page 43
1. to persuade the reader to wear
helmets when biking; 2. Every year,
153,000 people are taken to the
emergency room with bicycle-related
head injuries. 3. Answers will vary.
4. All helmets have ventilation holes
to let air through. A good helmet will
fit snugly but comfortably on the
head.; Helmets come in a variety of
styles and colors.; Even the most
experienced and alert bike riders
can take a tumble. Olympic bike
riders wear helmets.; There is a wide
range of prices for helmets.

Page 47
Possible answers: 1. Sagbata took
all of his mother's riches. He said the
wealth was his because he is the
oldest son. 2. Without the water that
Sogbo had, crops withered;
3. Sogbo's messenger was the
Wututu bird.